Homes around the world

Island Homes

Nicola Barber

Crabtree Publishing Company
www.crabtreebooks.com

Crabtree Publishing Company

www.crabtreebooks.com

Editors: Hayley Leach, Ellen Rodger, Michael Hodge
Senior Design Manager: Rosamund Saunders
Designer: Elaine Wilkinson
Geography consultant: Ruth Jenkins

Photo credits: Neil Cooper/Alamy p. 17;
Dinodia/Alamy p. 25; Robert Harding Picture Library
Ltd/Alamy p. 10, p. 27; Jeremy Hoare/Alamy p. 20; Craig
Lovell/Eagle Visions Photography/Alamy p. 14;
Nagelestock.com/Alamy cover and p. 12; Pat
Shearman/Alamy p. 11; Scottish Viewpoint/Alamy p. 24;
Chloe Harford/Corbis p. 19; Joson/zefa/Corbis p. 21;
Colin Prior/Corbis p. 22; Anders Ryman/Corbis p. 13;
Ron Chapple/Getty Images title page and p. 9; Paul
Chesley/Getty Images p. 8; Ryan McVay/Getty Images p.
15; Bruno Morandi/Robert Harding Picture Library/Getty
p. 6; Matthieu Paley/Getty Images p. 18; Jean
Pragen/Getty Images p. 16, p. 26; Colin Prior/Getty
Images p. 23; Karin Slade/Getty Images p. 7.

Cover: A group of colorful houses on
an island off Norway.

Title page: These homes are on the tiny island of Cebu,
in the Philippines.

Activity & illustrations: Shakespeare Squared
pp. 28, 29.

Because of the nature of the Internet, it is possible that
some website addresses (URLs) included in this book
may have changed, or sites may have changed or closed
down since publication. While the author and publisher
regret any inconvenience this may cause the readers, no
responsibility for any such changes can be accepted by
either the author or the publisher.

Library and Archives Canada Cataloguing in Publication

Barber, Nicola
Island homes / Nicola Barber.

(Homes around the world)
Includes index.
ISBN 978-0-7787-3543-4 (bound).--ISBN 978-0-7787-3555-7 (pbk.)

1. Island people--Dwellings--Juvenile literature. 2. Dwellings--
Juvenile literature. I. Title. II. Series: Barber, Nicola. Homes around the
world.

GN391.B37 2007   j392.3'609142   C2007-904711-4

Library of Congress Cataloging-in-Publication Data

Barber, Nicola.
Island homes / Nicola Barber.
p. cm. -- (Homes around the world)
Includes index.
ISBN-13: 978-0-7787-3543-4 (rlb)
ISBN-10: 0-7787-3543-5 (rlb)
ISBN-13: 978-0-7787-3555-7 (pb)
ISBN-10: 0-7787-3555-9 (pb)
1. Island people--Dwellings--Juvenile literature. 2. Island people--
Social life and customs--Juvenile literature. 3. Island ecology--Juvenile
literature. I. Title. II. Series.

GN391.B37 2008
392.3'609142--dc2   2007030182

Crabtree Publishing Company

www.crabtreebooks.com   1-800-387-7650

**Published in Canada
Crabtree Publishing**
616 Welland Ave.
St. Catharines, Ontario
L2M 5V6

**Published in the United States
Crabtree Publishing**
PMB16A
350 Fifth Ave., Suite 3308
New York, NY 10118

Published by CRABTREE PUBLISHING COMPANY
Copyright © **2008**

Contents

Words in **bold** can be found in the glossary on page 30

What is an island home?

An island is a piece of land that is surrounded by water. There are islands all over the world. Some people live on small islands that sit close to a larger piece of land, called the **mainland**.

▼ *Mont Saint Michel island is near to the mainland of France.*

Some islands are very big. For example, the country of Japan is made up of four large islands and more than 3,000 small islands! The British Isles has over 6,000 large and small islands.

▲ Japan is an island. Tokyo, Japan is one of the largest cities in the world.

Big and small islands

Many people live and work on islands. Some of them have homes in big cities, which are often crowded. Many people live on islands, far from other land, where there are not many people.

Island life
Some islands are so small that no one lives on them at all!

▲ *Manhattan Island in New York has tall buildings for homes and offices.*

Some islands are tiny, such as the Maldives in the Indian Ocean. There are 1,190 of these islands that cover just 186 **square miles** (300 square kilometers). The largest island in the world is Greenland. It covers 1.3 million square miles (2.16 million square kilometers).

▲ *These homes are on the tiny island of Cebu in the Philippines.*

Hot and cold islands

In hot places, people sometimes build their houses on **stilts**. The stilts raise the house off of the ground. This helps air circulate underneath to keep the houses cool. The stilts also help prevent snakes and other animals from going into the houses!

▼ This house on Flores, Indonesia, has windows with wooden bars to let air inside.

In places where the weather is wet and windy, or where there are few trees, houses are often built of stone. The stone walls keep the rain and wind out. Inside, the houses are dry and warm.

Island life

In many places, people make the roofs of their houses out of a grass. This is known as "thatch".

▲ *The small windows of this house in the Outer Hebrides of Scotland help prevent heat loss.*

Building an island home

People use a wide variety of **materials** to build their island homes. In large cities, tall buildings are made from **concrete**, **steel,** and glass. In small villages, people often build their houses from wood.

▼ *These brightly painted wooden houses are on an island in Norway.*

Islands are often located far away from other places. Island homes are made from **local** materials. People use **bricks** made out of earth or stones to build the walls of houses.

▲ *This woman on the Pacific island of Satawal is using leaves to make the roof of a house.*

Inside an island home

This home is on one of the islands of Fiji in the Pacific Ocean. It belongs to the chief of the village. It is decorated with special patterned cloths and white shells.

▼ *The mats on the floor have been made from local grasses.*

14

This family home is in Japan. The walls are made from light **bamboo** wood and thin **rice paper**. The floors are covered with mats made from straw.

▲ This family is sitting on the floor around a low table to eat a meal.

The weather

Islands around the world have different kinds of weather. Greenland is located in the north Atlantic Ocean where the weather is cold. There is snow and ice throughout the entire year.

▼ These homes are in Greenland. You can see ice floating on the water in the bay.

16

There are hundreds of small islands in the Caribbean Sea. These islands are hot and sunny. Every year from June to November, there is the danger of **hurricanes**.
A hurricane is a strong storm with very high winds and heavy rain.

Island life

In 2005, Hurricane Emily damaged over 2,500 homes on the Caribbean island of Grenada.

▲ *A hurricane damaged these homes on the Caribbean island of Jamaica.*

The environment

Over the years, the **sea level** around an island will change. When the sea level falls, you can see more of the **sea bed** around the island. When the sea level rises, water covers more of the land, and the island gets smaller.

▼ *These homes are on Tuvalu, an island in the Pacific Ocean. If sea levels rise, Tuvalu could disappear beneath the water.*

On some islands, there are **volcanoes**. When a volcano **erupts**, hot rock, called **"lava"**, flows onto the land around it. In 1995, a volcano erupted on the Caribbean sland of Montserrat. The island's Capital, Plymouth, was buried in ash and mud.

Island life
Tuvalu means "group of eight islands", but there are nine islands in the group!

▲ Volcano ash has almost completely covered this building on Montserrat in the Caribbean.

School and play

On small islands where there are not many people, school classes may have only a few pupils. If an island is close to the mainland, children may have to travel to the mainland to go to school.

▼ *This teacher is talking to her students in the Cook Islands in the Pacific Ocean.*

Children who live on islands often play on the beach and in the water. They learn to fish and swim. Sometimes they learn to sail a boat or dive down under the water to look at beautiful fish or **coral reefs**.

Island life

The most popular sport in the Caribbean islands is **cricket**.

▲ *These children are playing soccer on Kuta Beach in Bali, Indonesia.*

Going to work

Fishing is important for island people. Sometimes fishers sell the fish that they have caught to local stores and restaurants. Often, the fish are taken to other countries to be sold.

▼ *These fishers are unloading in the Seychelles, a group of islands off the east coast of Africa.*

Warm islands, such as the those in the Caribbean or Hawaii, are popular places for people to go on vacation. Many island people work in hotels or restaurants that are visited by tourists.

▲ *This woman sells her baskets to tourists on the island of Fiji in the Pacific Ocean.*

Getting around

On islands such as Great Britain, it is easy to travel around. There are good roads, railways and airports. Greenland is covered with ice and snow, so there are no railways and not many roads. People use helicopters and planes to travel between towns.

▼ *These people are going to fly on a small plane to get to the mainland of Scotland from the small island of Barra.*

People who live on small islands often use boats to travel to other islands, or the mainland. **Ferries** take passengers, as well as cars and other **vehicles**, from one island to another.

▲ *This ferry travels from the mainland of India at Goa to islands in the Mandovi river.*

Where in the world?

Some of the places mentioned in this book have been labeled here.

Look at these two pictures carefully.

- How are the homes different from each other?

- What is each home made of?

- Look at their walls, roofs, windows and doors.

- How are these homes different from where you live?

- How are they the same?

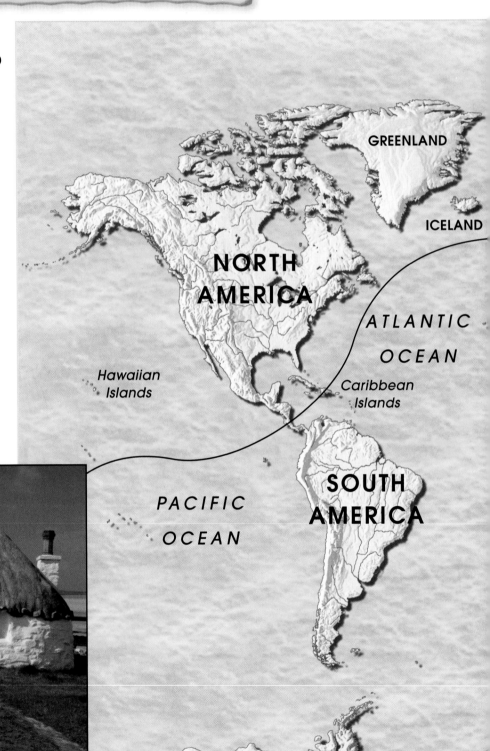

GREENLAND

ICELAND

NORTH AMERICA

ATLANTIC OCEAN

Hawaiian Islands

Caribbean Islands

PACIFIC OCEAN

SOUTH AMERICA

Outer Hebrides, Scotland

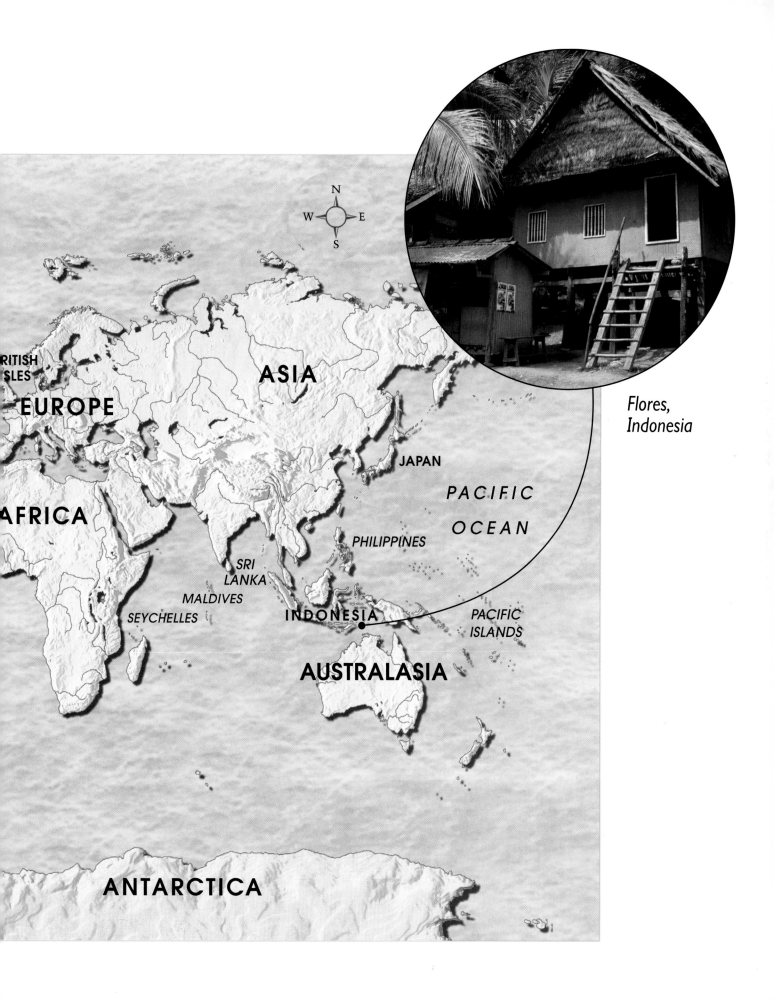

EUROPE

BRITISH ISLES

ASIA

AFRICA

JAPAN

PACIFIC OCEAN

PHILIPPINES

SRI LANKA

MALDIVES

SEYCHELLES

INDONESIA

PACIFIC ISLANDS

AUSTRALASIA

ANTARCTICA

N
W E
S

Flores, Indonesia

Island home for sale

Create a brochure to advertise the sale of an island home. Use the information in this book to help you.

What you need
- paper
- pencil
- pencil crayons or markers

1. Take another look at the pictures of island homes in this book. Choose one island home. This will be the home that you are trying to sell. Reread the information about this home.

2. Fold the sheet of paper in half, so the two shorter sides meet. This is your brochure. On the cover of the brochure, write "Island home for sale." You may decorate your cover, but do not draw a picture of your home here.

3. On the first inside page of the brochure, write a description of your home. To help you plan your writing, answer the questions below. You may also use this book to help you. Remember that you are trying to sell this home to people who have never visited it. You should try to use descriptive language that will convince them that they should buy it.

Questions to answer:

Where is this home?

What is this home made of?

What are some special features of this home?

How can people get to this home?

What is the price of this home?

4. On the other inside page, draw a picture of your island home. Make sure to draw the details that you included in your written description.

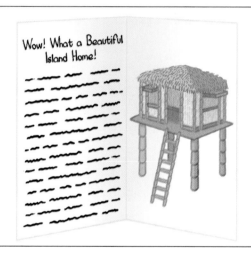

Compare and Contrast:

Look at the ads created by your classmates. How is yours different? How is yours the same? Which brochures are the most persuasive? Which home would you buy? Why? Discuss your answers with a classmate.

Glossary

bamboo	A kind of plant
brick	A hard block of mud and sand that is used for building
concrete	A mixture of cement, sand, and water that gets harder as it dries
coral reef	A hard, rocky material in warm seas that is made from the bodies of small underwater animals
cricket	A sport that is played between two teams with a small, hard ball and a wooden bat
erupt	When hot rocks are pushed violently from deep below the ground up to Earth's surface
ferry	A boat that carries people and vehicles from place to place
hurricane	A fierce storm with high winds and a lot of rain
lava	Hot rock and material that comes out of a volcano
local	Close to home or produced or living nearby
mainland	A large piece of land, rather than the islands around it
material	What something is made from
rice paper	Paper that is made from rice
sea bed	The bottom of the sea
sea level	The level of the sea around the world
square miles	The area covered by a square measuring a mile on each side
steel	A kind of metal that is very strong
stilts	Poles that are used to raise something off of the ground
tourist	A person who is on vacation
vehicle	Transportation with wheels, such as a car or a truck
volcano	A place where lava erupts from deep beneath Earth

Further information

Books to read

The Living Ocean series
Oceans, from the Nature Unfolds series
Oceans, and Volcanoes, from the Wonders of our World series
Nicola's Floating Home, from the Crabapples series
Cuba, Jamaica, Australia, Ireland, Japan, the Philippines, from the Lands, Peoples, and Cultures series

Websites

http://www2.hawaii.edu/~ogden/piir/
Pacific Islands Internet resource

http://www.greenland-guide.gl/
The official guide to Greenland

http://www.netstate.com/states/intro/hi_intro.htm
Information about Hawaii

http://www.japan-guide.com/list/e1000.html
Information about the geography of Japan

Index

All of the numbers in **bold** refer to photographs.

Printed in the USA